AUSTRALIAN PSALMS

Bruce D. Prewer

Lutheran Publishing House
Adelaide

National Library of Australia
Cataloguing-in-Publication data

Prewer, Bruce D.
Australian psalms.

ISBN 0 85910 075 8

1. Christian poetry, Australian. I. Title.

A821'.008031

Printed and published by
Lutheran Publishing House
205 Halifax Street, Adelaide, South Australia   L1900

To my
best friend:
Marie

Introduction

Until we discover God at work here in Australia, in the secular as well as the religious events, the Australian Church will not find itself and its destiny.

We 'down under' are oppressed by an insidious inferiority complex which makes us believe that the real events happen only on the other side of the world. We tend to think that the 'really real' things happened (and still happen) in Israel, Britain, and Europe; even in the USA a few real things occur! Everything in Australia seems 'less real' and therefore can't be taken as seriously. Our culture and our Christian sub-culture are dependent on the northern, largely-European scene. Theirs is the only real history; nothing ever really started to happen in Australia until Europeans came 200 years ago. Even the geography seems 'less real'; Ben Lomond or Mt Carmel, the fields of Devon, and the Rhine Valley seem 'more real' than Kosciusko or Cradle Mountain, the paddocks at Kingaroy, and the Derwent Valley.

If we are to throw off this cultural self-deprecation, we must see the Creator still at work here in Australia, as he has been from the beginning. But we won't see this until we begin to accept the Aboriginal culture and history as an authentic part of our history. We will not find ourselves until we humbly discover them as a profound part of the 'really real'.

The psalms in this book are a tiny, timid attempt to take God's Australia seriously in geographic terms. But they fail abysmally in historical terms because, to my shame, I am largely ignorant of the Aboriginal heritage. Perhaps the authentic Australian psalms will be written by our Aboriginals. Perhaps they are already composed, but our ears are switched off.

In this collection, in addition to my original psalms, there are a number of transpositions of biblical psalms. These are not translations. By 'transpositions' I mean that the setting is transposed from Israel to Australia, and from BC to AD times. For this reason, these psalms should not be read as a substitute for sound Bible translations. Nevertheless they are offered as material for worship, both public and private, just as they arose out of worship, both public and private.

Bruce Prewer,
March 1979

Contents

continued . . .

Part III: These Are the Days

PART I
The Sound of Joy

Everything That Draws Breath

God, our wonderful God, you make everything that delights
        the eye;
    Yours is the gift of everything that draws breath.

Yours is the energy that vibrates the wing of a bee,
    The gracefulness of black swans skimming over still lakes,
The joy of a puppy bounding to greet its owner,
    The courage of a shelduck leading ducklings to safe waters,
The song of a magpie on a soft spring morning,
    The beauty of pink galahs wheeling over trees at sunset,
The purpose in mutton birds returning to southern sand-hills,
    The warmth surrounding the joey in a kangaroo's pouch.

Yours, Creator God, is the skill of the wedge-tailed eagle,
    The play of the bandicoot on warm summer nights,
The strength of the baby koala clinging to its mother,
    The authority of seagulls riding salty winds,
The games of the dolphin surfing among swimmers,
    The communal chatter of colourful parrots,
The vigour of the trout leaping in quiet waters,
    The persistence of fairy penguins waddling up sandy slopes.

Yours, wonderful God, is the dance of the slender brolga,
    The industry of the ant through long summer days,
The power of the buffalo breaking through thickets,
    The glory on the radiant wings of a beetle,
The excitement of the platypus hunting for yabbies,
    The agility of mountain minnows darting between shaded rocks,
The wariness of the wallaby peeping from among bushes,
    The confidence of the sparrow winning crusts from pigeons.

Yours, Lord, truly yours, is the laughter of the kookaburra,
   The speed of an emu striding through mallee scrub,
The comedy of the crab side-scurrying over wet sand,
   The searching of the cockatoo for a place to nest,
The effortless padding of a dingo over saltbush plains,
   The conversation of the blackbirds at early morning,
The vision of the wombat as it rummages through long dark nights,
   The display of the lyre bird as he shares in creation's joy.

God, our wonderful God, you make everything that delights
     the eye;
   Yours is the gift of everything that draws breath!

Seals at Seal Bay, South Australia.

Reflection of the Unseen

Colossians 1

At the time when shadows were around us
and fears choked our joy,
You, most wonderful God, transferred us
into the kingdom of the Son of Love,
where there is the light
and liberty of the children of God.

Like the reflection of the sunrise
beaming over placid waters,
so is our Lord the true reflection
of you, our unseen God;
the beginning of all that was,
and the joyous completion
of all that is to be.

Our little planet
and the vast worlds in outer space
were spun by his power!
The things we see and discover,
and things no eye has seen
nor mind comprehended,
are all subject to his power
and filled with his purpose.

His ways are before all other.
The grace that coheres all things
is his and his alone.
The Church is his making
and he is its only head,
the first risen from all death,
the only Son to be named Lord.

Wonderful is your choice,
Most loving God,
to make the fullness of your nature
dwell in our True-Man Jesus,

reconciling the whole cosmos
to yourself through him,
bringing gracious peace
through that most bloody cross;
peace in time and eternity
through him alone.

Grace of Our Lord Jesus Christ

How shall we ever praise our Lord enough,
   Or serve him as he surely deserves?
His grace moves faster than light;
   His mercy is larger than the universe.

In every part of our home planet,
   Grace works without limit.
It saturates the weary centuries
   And fully fills each minute.

No nation is denied his grace
   Nor is any child outside it.
The cities and the farms partake alike;
   It works in lives that still deride it.

So deep that none can fall beneath it;
   In all the world no one is missed.
Our sins rise up, but ever higher
   His grace will rise and still persist.

What God's grace launched in Christ,
   Will one day be completed.
And though it suffer from a million blows,
   His grace will never be depleted.

Australian Accent

Brother, does the dust of Australia cling to your feet,
    as did the dust of Palestine?
Is your skin tanned like a jackeroo,
    and do you tend wounds in bush nursing hospitals?
Has Galilee become Lake St Clair or Jindabyne,
    and do fishermen still ferry you in their boats?

Brother, do you watch the crimson face of the waratah open,
    as you watched the lilies of the field?
Are you teaching us lessons from the kookaburra
    as you did from sparrows and ravens?
Do the wallaby and platypus delight you,
    providing a thought for an unforgettable text?

Brother, has Jericho moved to Alice Springs,
    and does Zacchaeus meet you under the river gums?
Have you walked through the wheatfields of the Mallee,
    or harvested with farmers at Parkes and Ceduna?
Do you tell stories to the cane workers at Bundaberg,
    or create parables from Barossa vineyards?

Brother, do you choose friends among the girls of Kings Cross,
    or make disciples from the drug-pushers of St Kilda?
When black people hold a wedding celebration,
    do you join them in corroboree?
When our migrant neighbours are abused,
    will you tell us the 'Parable of the Good Italian'?

Brother, what money-tables anger you today;
    are our cathedrals and churches dens of thieves?
Do Pilate and Herod still misgovern us,
    and are Australian crowds easily bought for Barabbas?
Do Pharisees or Sadducees now wear clerical collars,
    and does Caiaphas lobby for favours at Canberra?

Brother, do you pray at night in our bushland,
    or weep in the Gethsemane of our city parks?
Are you now betrayed by an Australian Judas,
    and deserted by your closest mates?
Have men become Peter and denied you
    in universities, pubs, and RSL clubs?

Brother, is the cross now made of scribbly gum,
    and do the nails come from Broken Hill?
Are you lifted up outside our cities
    and is Golgotha near every country town?

When you pray forgiveness on us all,
    isn't it an Australian accent that we hear?

Outback signposts, Queensland.

Jesus

Jesus, Son of Man,
   Jesus, Son of God,
radiance of the Father,
   first-born among many brothers:
to you belongs our sole allegiance
   and our everlasting gratitude!

When our world was ripe
   for despair or faith,
   you came to us.
With our uprooted hopes
lying fruitless around us,
   you shared our dust
   and planted a true vine
which shall ever be fruitful.

While proud and cultured men
   chased philosophical fashions,
   or created scribal absurdities,
You told unforgettable parables
   about farmers, servants, and wedding parties,
seeding the furrows of history
   with a potent Word bearing a harvest
   too vast for all the silos of this world.

In the terrible time of your dereliction,
when man attained his worst hour,
   you hung on that awful Cross
   bearing on tortured shoulders
   the sins of the whole world,
till in the gathering darkness
   you knew the task was done
   and the reconciliation begun.

In the light of Easter dawn,
    while disciples in whispers
    passed their despair one to another,
You arose at the call of the Father,
bringing light and immortality to light,
    warming hearts with inextinguishable joy,
    and rehabilitating doubters and deniers
with a love that overpowers the gates of hell.

Jesus, the Word made flesh,
    Jesus, friend of sinners,
Reconciler of the whole universe,
    the resurrection and the life:
Heaven and earth are full of your glory!
Our allegiance and gratitude are yours for ever!

Morning Sunlight

As the morning sun falls on tiled roof-tops
    and spreads warmth in east-west alleys,
My whole being rises to give praise;
    my every fibre rejoices in God.

Cars speeding on the freeway sparkle in light;
    in sunshine even the buses seem young again.
Already builders are at work on new houses,
    perched on rafters soaked with sunlight.
Laughing children skip their way to schoolgrounds,
    or pedal small bikes with spokes aflashing.
Across parks people short-cut to work —
    ladies stilt-stepping and men strong-striding.
Little children sun-dance to kinder,
    escorted by mothers, sisters, and brothers.
An old lady potters in her front garden;
    her husband promises the terrier a walk.
Overhead, gleaming planes jet interstate,
    while their teachers, the starlings, gather on power-lines.

Fruitcart, Rundle Mall, Adelaide.

Trains hoot through suburban crossings,
    and delivery vans begin their bustle.
Everything has wakened at the old sun's bidding;
    our whole city embraces a bright new day.

Blessed be your name, Giver of sunlight.
    Blessed be your name, Author of life.
Glory be to you, Lord of our city.
    Glory be to you, Renewer of life.

Happiness

Psalm 1

Happiness is the person who shuns unloving ways,
    who is not attracted by apathy or sarcasm,
But finds delight in Jesus' teaching,
    testing it out by day and by night.

Such people are like great red gums
    growing by the riverside;
Flowering every season, defying drought,
    and constantly putting forth new growth.

Not so unloving people;
    they are like grass in a willy-willy.
When pressure is on they can't take it,
    nor can they stand the company of good folk.

Those who love have their tap-roots in God;
    the unloving are rootless.
The Lord can work with loving people,
    but the unloving work their own ruin.

The Ways of God
Psalm 19

The Southern Cross signals God's glory;
    the Milky Way gleams with his handiwork.
Every new day tells his story;
    at night-time his skills are displayed.
All nations and tongues can understand his language;
    his message saturates our planet.
Look at the merry old sun in his robes of light;
    he smiles like a bridegroom on his wedding day.
Keen as an athlete at the Olympics,
    he strides from Sydney to Perth.
Then he sprints the other half of the circuit,
    missing no nation with his warmth.

How complete are the ways of the Lord,
    constantly restoring our humanity.
He is a dependable counsellor,
    with wisdom for those who have open minds.
The Lord's purposes are beautiful,
    making our heart leap with joy.
His commands are clear,
    bringing a new light into our eyes.
The respect he arouses is healthy,
    extending for ever.
His assessment of us is fair,
    completely to be trusted.
His word is more valuable than a fortune,
    more precious than reserves of gold.
It is sweeter than the finest confectionery,
    more natural than the honey of mallee blossom.
It keeps your servants alert and sensitive;
    living by it brings us incomparable gain.

If we should think he has made mistakes,
    it's time to check our own motives.
Save your servants from self-conceit,
    from the deadly reign of ego.

Then shall we live without shame,
　　free from the worst of all treason.
May these words tumbling from the mouth,
　　and the feelings surging in the heart,
Be acceptable in your eyes,
　　dear Lord, our true strength and our Saviour.

Familiar Things

Sing from the mountain-tops and shout to the skies!
   Praise him all his messengers, and cheer him all his servants!
Let the whole of our continent praise the Lord:
   mountain and desert, river, waterfall, and farmland.
Let the vegetation praise the Lord:
   gum tree and wattle, blackboys, boronia, and lotus lily.
Let all animals praise the Lord:
   koala and kangaroo, Tasmanian devil, possum, and wombat.
Let the birds of plain and forest praise the Lord:
   galah and emu, blue wren, honeyeater, and jabiru.
Let coastland and seas praise the Lord:
   surf and tides, beaches, coral, and rock-pool.
Let everything in the seas praise the Lord:
   seal and penguin, starfish, snapper, and dolphin.
Let our cities take time to praise the Lord:
   park and street, housewife, garbage-man, and councillor.
Let all music praise the Lord:
   guitar and organ, orchestra, pop-group, and didgeridoo.
Let everything living under the sun,
   everything that is or ever will be,
   praise the Lord! Hallelujah!

Brushtailed possums,
Queensland.

Exuberant Praise

Psalm 148

Cheer the Lord, everyone!
  Everything, praise him!

Cheer him from our skies;
  praise him from outer space.
Cheer him, you astronauts;
  praise him, all children of the stars.
Cheer him, sun and moon;
  praise him, all distant galaxies.
Cheer him, all who are close to his heart;
  praise him, all mysteries beyond our knowledge.
All of you, cheer the Lord,
  for he speaks and you come into being.
He gives you a place for ever;
  He fixes the universal laws.

Cheer the Lord from this planet earth:
  rolling ocean and powerful hurricane;
Lightning, hail, snow, and ice;
  wind and storm fulfilling his purposes;
Our mountains, plains, and hills;
  our orchards, cane-fields, and forests;
Kangaroo, possum, and platypus;
  lizard and snake, black swan and rosella parrot.

Prime ministers and presidents of the earth;
  Cabinet ministers and high court judges;
Exuberant teenagers,
  old people and children,
Come on, all of you, cheer the Lord;
  he alone is worth it!
His glory transfigures this earth,
  and blazes from a million suns.
He has given mankind high honour;
  heroes will applaud his faithfulness.
Those who trust his presence will shout:
  'Cheer the Lord!'

The Bountiful God

Psalm 104

With all my being I celebrate the Lord!
  My wonderful God, you are dressed in glorious love!
You come to us as bright as the sunlight,
  and signal to us out of the star-flecked sky.
You refresh us with rain and play on tumbling clouds,
  and ride on the wings of the wind.
The breezes are your messengers,
  and the sparkling fire is your servant.

In the first travail of our planet's birth,
  while earth's crust settled and seas found their shores,
While mountains stood tall and valleys nestled below,
  you were present with a word insistent as thunder.
You were the one who first poured streams down valleys,
  letting the kangaroo drink and the cockatoo quench his thirst.
You saw the kookaburra settle in the scrub,
  laughing from among the branches,
While the mountain ash lifted high its head,
  and the river gums gave nesting place to the owl and parrot.

Even now you are still at work;
  on the rocky hills you shelter the wallaby and lizard.
The farmers look up as the clouds still give sweet rain,
  so that the grass grows and the sheep and cattle are fed.
Over the wheat crops the showers spread,
  the thirsty vineyards are watered;
On the slopes the banana plantations are refreshed,
  till the face of man shines with happiness.

Your sun and moon revolve on,
  regulating all waking and sleeping;
After dark the wild creatures are on the move,
  then at dawn they slink back to their lairs.
In the rhythm of this good life man gets up to work;
  tired, he comes home at night and receives rest.

Lord, everything you do is so bountiful!
    The wide sea swarms with tuna, prawns, and mackerel.
The world teems with living things, all depending on you,
    taking what you offer, feeding from your hands.
If you should hide your face, fear would overtake us;
    if you should withdraw your breath, all would be no more.
But you would only have to speak and all would be renewed;
    the face of the earth would be radiant again.

May your rule last for ever!
    May you always find joy in your precious planet!
We tremble with joy at your glance!
    We come to life at your touch!

Wheatfields, Western Australia.

Joys of Home Life

Let us praise the Lord for his goodness:

For our homes of the past and homes of today,
precious memories and present joys.
    Hallelujah, hallelujah!

For the intimate fun of family celebrations,
the enrichment of guests at our family meal.
    Hallelujah, hallelujah!

For the cries and cooing of a first baby,
the thrill of watching a child become adult.
    Hallelujah, hallelujah!

For little people chatting with make-believe presences,
and dolls, scooters, finger-paintings, and birthdays.
    Hallelujah, hallelujah!

For pets that make our home their own —
dogs, guinea-pigs, cats, and budgies.
    Hallelujah, hallelujah!

For familiar walls holding out a storm,
and chairs and beds which have 'our feel' about them.
    Hallelujah, hallelujah!

For the shared excitement of planning things new,
and sorrowing together when things go wrong.
    Hallelujah, hallelujah!

For the love which allows us to be irritable with each other,
weakness accepted and strengths shared.
    Hallelujah, hallelujah!

For fragile ties which hold under strain,
forgiveness sought and forgiveness given.
    Hallelujah, hallelujah!

For our homes of today and homes yet to come,
present joys and hopes for tomorrow,
    Hallelujah, hallelujah, hallelujah!

A New Song
Psalm 98

Come, sing a new song to God,
    for he has worked wonders!

With the strength of redeeming love
    he is saving creation.
He has brought his actions into the open,
    showing his love to all nations.
He has not forgotten his servants of old
    to whom he was so loyal;
But now every country on earth
    shall see what our God is doing.

Join the celebrations everyone,
    shout and sing for joy!
Praise God with the guitar;
    add your voice to the strings.
Join in with trumpet and drums
    till a joyful noise greets our King.
Let the sea roar and everything in it,
    the land and everything on it.
Come on, rivers, clap your hands,
    and you mountains, join the choir!

For the Lord comes to govern our planet,
    to deal out a new kind of justice,
And to make mercy his rule.

Faith, Hope, and Love

Faith like a mustard seed,
Power so small:
Word growing into deed,
Reaching tall,
Gift for all.

Hope making all things new,
Vision grand:
Christ's dream which shall come true,
In our land,
Near at hand.

Love larger than the world,
Christ's new song:
Power from which death recoiled,
Love so strong,
We belong.

Faith, hope, and love are free,
Boundless store;
New heaven and earth shall be
Without flaw,
Evermore.

This may be sung to the opening horn call from Schubert's Symphony in C, 'The Great'

Christians Together

Give praise to God who joins us here,
Whose healing Spirit casts out fear:
    Hallelujah, hallelujah!
Let each our neighbour's joy partake,
And to our God thanksgiving make.
    O praise him, O praise him,
    Hallelujah, hallelujah, hallelujah!

Give praise to God who gives us Christ,
Whose love redeems a mighty host:
    Hallelujah, hallelujah!
Let each our neighbour's faith uphold,
And to our God our joy be told.
    O praise him, O praise him,
    Hallelujah, hallelujah, hallelujah!

Give praise to God whose Spirit leads,
To serve mankind in all its needs:
    Hallelujah, hallelujah!
Let each our neighbour's hope repair,
And to our God all joy now share.
    O praise him, O praise him,
    Hallelujah, hallelujah, hallelujah!

This may be sung to the tune, *Lasst uns erfreuen*.

Slightly Less than Gods

Psalm 8

God, our God, yours is the most wonderful name in all the world,
    the highest joy in the whole universe!
Little children know this and grow strong;
    rebellious adults break themselves against your truth.
I see your fingers at work in vast galaxies;
    sun and moon obey you to the very second.
I can't help wondering why you remember mankind,
    why you bother about creatures like us.
Yet you have made us only slightly less than gods,
    trusting us with remarkable responsibility.
You have asked us to take charge of our land,
    making all other creatures subject to our authority:
The cattle and sheep, the kangaroo and crocodile,
    wedge-tailed eagle, magpie, and cockatoo,
Barramundi, tuna, dolphin, and shark,
    turtles, fairy penguins, and seals.
O God, our dear God,
    yours is the most astounding name in all the world!

Most s-w tip of Australia, Cape Leeuwin, Western Australia.

For Things That Go Well

In a world where many things go wrong,
  we praise you, God, for things that go well:
Marriages that are sound and beautiful,
  each person nurtured in respect and love.
Grandparents who share the make-believe of children,
  and grandchildren who love deeply in response.
Families where there is no generation-gap,
  where members can be together or apart without fuss.

We praise you for natural things taken for granted,
  the normal rhythm of continuing creation:
Trees that purify the polluted air,
  breathing in our waste and giving us oxygen.
The robust old sun that never rests,
  encouraging up from the earth our daily bread.
The never-failing power of water to quench our thirst —
  and a dozen tasty drinks dependent on it.

We praise you, God, for national parks,
  where kangaroo will not hide from man;
For places where parrots will share our picnics,
  and kookaburras laugh from nearby trees;
Lakes which mirror sunrise and sunset,
  home for duck, ibis, and leaping fish;
Protected forests where lyre-birds still display;
  and for desert flowers, celebrating for countless years.

We praise you for folk who love their neighbours,
  genuinely looking for no reward.
For much-criticized churches which still keep going,
  treasuring the Gospel in spite of the cynics.
For the influence of that matchless Jesus,
  the best name in our prayers since childhood.
For the unearned times of courage, joy, love, and light,
  when your grace becomes our joy.

His Works around Us

Psalm 147

What joy it is to sing hymns to our God!
   Praise is a sheer delight!
The Lord is rebuilding Australia;
   he is gathering the homeless people of the world.
He heals the broken-hearted,
   and bandages their wounds.

This is the same God who knows every star;
   he has a name for each planet and moon.
Powerful beyond all imagining is he;
   no computer can process his wisdom.
This wonderful Lord lifts up the meek;
   he throws the arrogant to the ground.
Sing a hymn of thanksgiving to the Lord!
   Let all melody and harmony give praise to our God!

It is he who fills the summer sky with clouds,
   preparing rain for the parched earth.
He clothes the hills with a garment of green,
   and supplies juice in the fruit of our orchards.
On cattle stations the animals find feed,
   even wild budgerigars get their share.
In winter the fleecy snowfields are his gifts,
   and crisp frosts express his laws.
Icicles are his delicate sculpture;
   frozen lakes lie still at his bidding.
Then at his wish the ice is melted;
   the warm winds blow and the rivers flow.

The Lord is not impressed with our technology;
   nor has he pleasure in strong-arm tactics.
His pleasure is in those who respect him,
   who trust their lives to his love.
Honour the Lord, you Australians!
   Praise him from Darwin to Hobart!
For he offers new possibilities to all our people,
   and blessings on all our children.

He has given us a country at peace,
  with more food than we can eat.
His laws can be relied on in every situation;
  his Word is faster than sound.
To our pioneers he made known his Word;
  his love and justice are proclaimed in our land.

No nation has fared better than Australia —
  yet is his rule accepted in many hearts?
O sing to the Lord a new song!
  Let the whole nation praise the Lord!

Never Alone

Psalm 139

Lord, you see right through me,
   and know me utterly.
You understand what I'm thinking,
   long before I understand myself.
You are with me on the crowded street;
   beside me when I go alone to bed.
Everything I do, you recognize;
   my tongue never wags without you hearing.
I find you in my yesterdays and tomorrows,
   your love firmly around me.
All this is too much for me;
   It is beyond my understanding.

Where could I evade you?
   Where could I escape your presence?
If I live high with the jet-set, you are there.
   If I make my bed on a park bench, you are there.
If I could take off at the speed of light
   and travel the freeways of outer space,
Even there your hand would touch me,
   your right hand would hold me.
If I fear something awful will happen,
   like being swallowed by darkness,
My darkness will begin to shine like the day;
   for with you darkness becomes light.

How precious are your plans for me, Lord;
   they add up to a fantastic number.
If I tried to count them
   they would outnumber the sand.
Whenever I wake up to what's happening
   I find I'm still with you!
Lord, take a hard look at me;
   untangle my untidy motives.
Sort me out with your relentless mercy;
   weigh up all my ideas.
Tear away whatever is unloving in me,
   and lead me into your never-ending future.

The Wind

Like the wind swaying through mountain trees,
    Or surging through thickets of wattle,
So, Lord, is your presence with us;
    Your power thrusts through our lives.
You sweep away our petty worries
    And shake us free from fears.
At your pressure we move and sway together,
    As if we were of one mind.

Sometimes you are as strong as winter storms,
    At others as soft as the rustling of ferns.
We are taught to bend and not be broken,
    To be flexible without shifting ground.
You test the strength of our feet
    And whatever proves shallow is uprooted.

On calm days we rest content,
    Glad to watch each other in stillness;
Enjoying quietness because we know
    You are still with us.

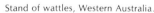

Stand of wattles, Western Australia.

Father of the Lights

The Letter of James

Father of the lights of heaven,
God of the faith that works:
    Every good gift you present to us,
    unchanging legacies you give us.
    Not in passing moods
    but in calculated love
    you offer us a new vision
    through Jesus, Prince of light.

Father of the lights of heaven,
God of the faith that works:
    When our wisdom crumbles,
    you bring us true insight —
    uncomfortable yet comforting,
    costly yet absolutely free!
    Bonus-God, you never ignore
    or rebuff the child who asks.

Father of the lights of heaven,
God of the faith that works:
    Your brand of wisdom is practical,
    it is cheerful and merciful,
    rich in compassionate deeds
    and the foe of empty words.
    There is no longer room for blame,
    for the Lord is full of compassion.

Father of the lights of heaven,
God of the faith that works:
    Happy are those who remain true!
    Happy are the inheritors of your grace!
    They possess the promised gift,
    the large love of God,
    where widows and orphans are treasured
    more than crowns and fortunes!

Astounding God

Astounding God!
Today I want to praise you
for amazing grace:

finding without seeking . . .
possessing without keeping . . .
the end where the beginning begins . . .
good news that is offensive . . .
doubting which is believing . . .
uselessness which is most useful . . .
the word that is speechless . . .
the death which dies . . .
poverty which owns the universe . . .
memory that looks forward . . .
emptiness which overflows . . .
bread which creates hunger . . .
mystery that is unmistakable . . .
the folly which is wisdom . . .
the Cross which is glory . . .
the God who is a servant.

For amazing grace
today I want to praise you!
Astounding God!

Worship in a Caravan Park

For the sounds of this summer morning:
    call of finches in the surrounding scrub,
    incessant vibration of innumerable insects,
    flopping of thongs as a camper goes by,
    song of a magpie in a bare-limbed tree,
    rattle of breakfast dishes from caravans,
    gossip of sparrows at play in the dust,
    chatter of two children in holiday glee,
    and the background roar of the restless sea:
I thank you, Creator Spirit.

For the sights of this holiday morning:
    two grey herons on the flanks of the river,
    distant effervescence of breaking waves,
    colourful towels drying in the breeze,
    tangled-haired surfer eager for his fun,
    regiment of seagulls ranked on a spit,
    small boy carrying milk to his tent,
    rhythm of joggers on their morning run,
    and swallows glistening in the shining sun:
I thank you, Creator Spirit.

For the smells of this summer morning:
    sweet fragrance of tea-tree blossom,
    unmistakable odour of seaweed,
    aroma of toast, coffee, and tea,
    smell of salt in the wind so clean,
    fumes of oil from an outboard motor,
    scent of coconut from sunburn cream,
    and the smell of cormorants perched upstream:
I thank you, Creator Spirit.

For the feel of this holiday morning:
    bare legs warming in summer sun,
    supporting contours of a strong beach chair,
    awareness of belonging to land, sea, and sky,
    delight of breathing unpolluted air,

feel of sand between one's toes,
hand of a loved one sharing the joys,
freedom from duties and every care,
and the soft breeze caressing cheek and hair:
I thank you, Creator Spirit.

The Voice of God
Psalm 29

Give yourselves to the Lord, children of God!
    Give to the Lord all power and glory!
Offer him the praise his name deserves!
    Worship him with wholeness of life!

The voice of the Lord is stronger than rushing streams;
    above the thundering surf of the oceans he speaks.
Listen to the mighty word of the Lord;
    filled with majesty is his message.
His voice could splinter Tasmanian blue gums;
    the cedars of New England would shatter in pieces.
At his word mountains would leap like the wallaby,
    Kosciusko and the Cradle like the red kangaroo.
If the Lord commanded it, Ayers Rock would split,
    torn asunder as from fierce fire.
The voice of the Lord whips up the Gibson Desert;
    he whirls the Simpson into red dust storms.
When he speaks, forest giants are uprooted,
    or the mulga scrub is stripped bare.
Those who live close to him are in awe,
    while everything shouts 'Glory!'

From the very beginning, the Lord alone is King;
    his government is established for ever.
Lovingly he gives strength to his people;
    in his blessing is our joy and peace.

Our City

King of the City not made with hands,
    Lord of the New Jerusalem,
We thank you for our worldly city,
    We praise you for our populous home.

For office blocks and slender skyscrapers,
    And the sturdy architecture of our forebears;
For busy streets and crowded lanes,
    Government House and city squares:
        We thank you, Lord.

For lunch-hour bustle and Friday rush;
    Window-shopping when things close down;
For city arcades with little shops;
    Large emporium and shopping-town:
        We thank you, Lord.

For cricket ground and sun-browned crowd,
    Golf course, bowling alley, and hockey field;
For lovely parks, fountains, and flowers,
    Botanical gardens with trees of the world:
        We thank you, Lord.

For street-sweepers toiling while we sleep;
    Policemen untangling a traffic snarl;
For garbage collectors and their chugging trucks,
    Fire engines with sirens all awail:
        We thank you, Lord.

For water in taps, piped from the hills;
    Buses at our stop and trains at the station;
For electricity at the switch and gas in the heater;
    Evening newspapers with news of our nation:
        We thank you, Lord.

For the rich variety of films and plays,
   Visits of ballet and opera stars;
For symphony orchestras and massed choirs,
   Pop concerts and twang of guitars:
     We thank you, Lord.

For churches, Sunday-schools, and clubs,
   The vaulted cathedral with tall steeple;
For divine gifts in limitless patterns,
   And the face of Jesus in countless people:
     We thank you, Lord.

Sydney Harbour and Opera House.

Baptism

Lord, we stand awed
in the presence of your evangelist:
this tiny baby thing who dares
to be your child!

Not one word can she speak,
this your little messenger;
yet in the silence she declares
the living Word!

She has no prior faith
and brings no creed or prayer,
but from this font she bears
the faith of Christ!

She offers now no promises
nor deeds of righteousness,
but here receives and shares
the righteousness of God!

Helpless, she comes today,
carried in the arms of others,
yet in her helplessness she wears
your massive strength!

Lord, this is the greatest thing:
here a child has Brother, Friend,
and a Father who cares
world without end!

Holy Communion

I have visited Bethlehem's sacred site,
trod the worn stones of the ancient square,
from the shepherds' fields I saw the sun go down
and watched the guiding stars appear —
    but my Lord was not especially there.

In Nazareth's streets there were children at play,
and carpenters laughed as they made a repair,
the market was decked with bright garments and fruits,
while old men washed feet for their midday prayer —
    but my Lord was not especially there.

I have walked on the banks of Galilee,
listened to the waves on its pebbly shore,
seen shepherds guide flocks beside still waters,
and heard fishermen's voices on the morning air —
    but my Lord was not especially there.

On streets of Jerusalem were cascades of people,
barrows, donkeys, and porters with loads to bear;
I rejoiced on Mount Zion, in Gethsemane whispered,
and to an upper room climbed by a well-worn stair —
    but my Lord was not especially there.

In a tiny church under an Australian sun,
the farmlands shimmering with summer glare,
I've knelt with a few other ordinary souls
round a Table spread with the simplest fare —
    and truly my Lord was especially there.

The Divine Secret

Ephesians 1

> To the God and Father of our Lord Jesus Christ,
>> Let our honour and praise be joyfully given!
> In Christ the supreme blessings of eternity
>> Are lavished on the children of time and dust!

Before the creation of the universe began,
  Before our planet received its shape and colour,
When tree had not yet grown nor bird sung,
  He planned us to be his special creatures,
To become complete without any flaw,
  Overflowing with the gift of love.

> Great and marvellous are your deeds,
>> King of all ages!
> Beautiful are the works of your fingers,
>> Lord of the beginning and the end!

It was his secret purpose and joy
  Through the power of the lovely Christ,
To destine us to become his own children,
  Releasing love and praise in all places.
For our liberation and fulfilment is certain
  Through the shedding of the blood of the Beloved.

> Wonderful is the name of Jesus Christ,
>> Father of all mercy!
> Beautiful is the voice that brings our freedom,
>> God of liberty!

Through the life of Jesus, freely offered,
  All our sins have been forgiven;
We see the wealth of amazing grace
  Poured upon us without limit,
Bringing a knowledge greater than all learning,
  And insight deeper than all sages and prophets.

Who shall not marvel at your wisdom,
    God of our salvation!
Who shall not tremble at the cost,
    Father of the Crucified!

The Divine secret, so long obscured,
    Prepared from the beginning in Christ,
Has now been shown openly to us,
    Implemented when the time was ripe:

Everything, absolutely everything in the universe,
    In the expanses of eternity and the confines of time,
Is to be brought into a glorious harmony
    Through the Christ, our incomparable Lord!

Glorious is your secret,
    Reconciling God!
Let prophets, apostles, and martyrs,
    And everything in earth and heaven,
Exult with unbounded joy
    From generation to generation, evermore!

Reflections, Wynyard Lake, Tasmania.

Who Am I?

I am the joyful shepherds
   who heard the angels sing —
And the preoccupied innkeeper
   whose stable housed a King.

I am the three wise men
   who travelled from afar —
And the terrible King Herod
   who feared your rising star.

I am the disciples who followed
   the new friend they had found —
And the fussy scribes who found you
   too uncomfortable to have around.

I am the prodigal son
   come home to my Father's place —
And the righteous elder brother
   who resented the gift of grace.

I am the rich man who lived it up,
   spurning the beggar at the gate —
And bustling, touchy Martha,
   who couldn't bear to sit and wait.

I am the crowd that gathered,
   wanting to put a crown on your head —
And I am the devil who tempted you
   with pleas for power, signs, and bread.

I am Zacchaeus who unprepared
   had you as guest and Saviour —
and the stiff-necked Pharisees
   who grumbled about your behaviour.

I am the crowd who cried 'Hosanna' —
    And Peter who let you down;
The police who did their duty well,
    and laughed at your thorny crown.

I am John who stood near your cross —
    And the soldiers who nailed the wood;
Mary who found an empty tomb —
    and Thomas, a risen Lord!

I am the apostles who took your Gospel
    to people everywhere.
Lord, I am just one hungry child
    with bread to eat and to share.

Jesus Is King

Come, join to praise with morning light:
    Our loving King!
Let grateful voices sound with might:
    Our loving King!
Let children's voices tell their praise,
While aged lips extol your ways,
Let every tongue in joy unite:
    Our loving King
    To you we bring
    Our praise!

Let songs like this ring through our land:
    Our loving King!
From coastal farms and inland sand:
    Our loving King!
Let all our nation thankful raise
Its voice in glad tumultuous praise:
    Our loving King
    To you we bring
    Our praise!

Let earth's great millions thund'rous shout:
    Our loving King!
Let this song spin the clouds about:
    Our loving King!
We'll always shout and sing your praise
While years flit by like passing days,
Until time runs its last hour out:
    Our loving King
    To you we bring
    Our praise!

PART II
The Shame and the Glory

Holiness

I saw the Lord
weeping
with Aboriginal mothers
around shanties
and reservations
where children learn little
except early death
or from their fathers
the way of despair
and toxic bitterness —
    weeping.

   Holy, holy, holy is the Lord of hosts;
   The whole earth is full of his glory.

I saw the Lord
gasping
for breath in those churches
wherever shallow worshippers
mouth blessing on the hungry
then drive home
to overfills of protein
and sport on the TV —
    gasping.

   Holy, holy, holy is the Lord of hosts;
   The whole earth is full of his glory.

I saw the Lord
hoping
in students scanning open books
roughly asking why
why
why
searching deep into friendly eyes
for seeds of truth
worth living for
and dying —
    hoping.

Holy, holy, holy is the Lord of hosts;
The whole earth is full of his glory.

I saw the Lord
agonizing
through corridors and chambers
of Canberra
where hollow men
salute expediency
consult the opinion polls
so that our future
will be the past repeated
spreading stench like the last —
    agonizing.

Holy, holy, holy is the Lord of hosts;
The whole earth is full of his glory.

I saw the Lord
angry
whenever church councils and committees
tardily
face agenda lifelessly
with no fire in the gut
no hope in the eye
no readiness to lose all
in the Kingdom which
comes first —
    angry.

Holy, holy, holy is the Lord of hosts;
The whole earth is full of his glory.

O Lamb of God, who takes away the sins of the world,
    Have mercy upon us.
O Lamb of God, who takes away the sins of the world,
    Have mercy upon us.
O Lamb of God, who takes away the sins of the world,
    Grant us your peace.

Penitence

We watch and wait, Lord,
   we scan the horizon for a sign of change —
Like farmers in a year of drought,
   looking for a change of heart in Australia.
For our countrymen have become like crows;
   like scavengers that live off the disasters of others;
Like hawks hovering,
   looking for smaller creatures to devour.

They care not for the exploited or unemployed,
   their only interest is in their own pay-packet.
Big business is as rapacious as a pack of dingoes;
   strong unions lie in wait like the crocodile.
Survival of the fattest is the national creed;
   little people are the ones who bleed.

Tanks and windmill, New South Wales.

We scorn the land rights of Aborigines,
    and admit a minimum of refugees.
People of low ability are labelled bludgers;
    loyal men in their fifties are declared redundant.
New Australians are given the dirtiest jobs;
    and their culture is mocked and despised.
Overseas aid is tied to political strings;
    we gamble a million times more than we give to the poor.

Lord, we wait and watch for change of heart,
    torn by anger and grief at ourselves and others.
We, the ugly Australians, pray for salvation,
    for the Rain that can make our centre bloom again.
We, the sick Australians, pray for healing,
    for the Prescription that can cure our festering sores.

How Long?

Psalm 13

How long will it be, Lord, before you remember me?
    How long will you remain incognito?
How long must I daily grieve and suffer inwardly?
    How long shall my opponents crow over me?

Look at me, Lord, and give me an answer;
    let me see some light, or I might as well be dead.
My opponents will consider me defeated,
    laughing when they watch me tremble.

Yet I will still trust your mercy,
    celebrating in my heart your salvation,
Singing to the true God
    who has been more than generous to me.

Rebellion

Some days we find it hard to love you, Lord;
 we smoulder with rebellion, even in church.
Your way of managing this world seems wrong;
 your love and justice appear to be missing.
From Ireland to Cambodia, Australia to Chile,
 we confront a tangle of suffering.
From New York to Peking, Canberra to Moscow,
 there is no clear path that leads to a better world.
The world shudders with injustice and torture;
 hatreds and fear spawn the agony of wars.
All the efforts of nobler people bear poor fruit;
 prophets, seers, and poets die unfulfilled.
Well-meaning politicians are reduced to cynicism;
 their ideals perish under the weight of 'respectable' corruption.
Scientific discoveries are prostituted by pride, greed, and war;
 even gifted physicians serve the rich rather than the sick.

It seems your fault, Lord!
 You made this world where tragedies occur!
Why did you create the possibility of greed?
 Or the neglect of your Aboriginal children?
The neuroses that afflict high-rise living?
 And the stupidity of poker machines and the road toll?
You permitted the opening for graft and corruption;
 you allow injustice and starvation to continue.
In us you have placed a hunger for a better world,
 but we lack the ability to build that world.
None of us are able to put into practice all we believe;
 you let us wander among our broken promises.
Lord, to whom can we turn?
 Where can we find adequate resources?

Lord, if it were not for Jesus of Nazareth,
 we would have given up long ago.
If his forgiveness and renewal were removed,
 we would slip away into dark despair.

But because you have given us one proper man
   in whom salvation takes glorious shape,
There is hope for us all,
   there is joy at the end of the travail.
O let our lives become filled with his grace!
   Weld our souls to the steel of his soul!
Transform our rebellion into renewed discipleship;
   replace our anger with a fresh discipline.
Help us to see your love at work in darkest places,
   and to recognize your glory in tiny victories!
O lead us into the new creation begun in Jesus!
   Raise up your new nation among all nations!

Homes

Psalm 127

Unless home-life is built by the Lord,
   the carpenter's efforts are useless;
Unless a nation trusts in God,
   armies are quite worthless.
To work heavy overtime,
   or to run two jobs at once
in order to get rich quickly,
   is an exercise in futility.
For the Lord supplies our deepest needs,
   and his gifts are as free as sleep.

Children are a favour from the Lord,
   a family the loveliest reward.
Better than weapons to a soldier
   are children to godly parents;
They are indeed a happy couple
   who are hugged daily by tiny arms.
They shall never feel defeated
   when doubts and fears assail them.

The Still Centre

When we want healing at the core of being,
    we turn to you, God of Christ Jesus!
When we discover the still centre of the storm,
    it's you we find there, most wonderful Lord!

Sometimes our life seems a jumble of fragments;
    nothing matches nor fits together.
A feeling of being lost floods in like a tide;
    anxiety erodes our inmost selves.
We are permeated by seeping discomfort,
    as if we are at odds with our own soul.
All good humour hides itself away;
    peace and joy become mere memory.

Then it is we find it hard to care for others;
    we are too distracted to notice their needs.
Self-giving becomes an impossible calling;
    love shrinks into a four-letter word.
Even our capacity to listen closes down;
    our counsel is but jagged lumps of yesterday.

Ayers Rock, Northern Territory.

Father of Christ, we refind ourselves only in you;
nowhere else do we find true integration.
At home with you we are at home with ourselves;
in your love we begin to care for ourselves.
Your peace passes all understanding;
your joy liberates the laughter within us.
We begin to hear, and care for others again;
love is shared as from a depthless source.
How shall we thank you, most loving God?
Can gratitude ever find adequate voice?
Still Centre of all the storms, we worship you!
Crux of the universe, we glorify you!

The Only Hope

Psalm 5

Lord, you hear what I'm saying;
you see what I'm thinking.
My only hope is for you to keep listening;
you're the only One to whom I can turn.
Every morning my tongue feels for the best words;
when I wake up I want to praise you.
You don't find pleasure in our mistakes;
for nothing unloving can live with you.
Stupidity cannot stand up to you;
those who hurt others shall taste your displeasure.
For my part, I will come to church celebrating your love;
in gratitude I'll turn my face to the Table and the Cross.
Lead me, Lord, in genuine goodness;
show me the way which goes straight ahead.
Come, everyone who loves God, celebrate with me;
join me in a shout of joy!
You care for them too;
may they find utter happiness in you.
For you give happiness to all loving people;
your caring love is stronger than steel.

When We Are Feeling Down

Hey, everyone! Celebrate the Lord with me!
    Join in, all you people who are feeling down!
Today is a time for affirming life,
    each hour a commitment in hope.
When we are feeling low, that is the time for praise;
    when our feelings mock us, our mind should give thanks.

On some days it is easy to worship,
    for love and gratitude arrive eagerly,
Bringing heart-warming joy,
    like children coming to a party.
Such praise is as native as the grevillea;
    as natural as mallee blossom in springtime.

But there are other days when we see only the shadows:
    the grime on buildings, the papers in gutters,
The cat stalking the blackbird,
    the wind tearing a limb from the red gum,
The politician's absurd duplicity,
    the unionist's stupidity and the businessman's greed.
Music on the radio is banal and absurd,
    while newspapers headline the horrible;
Even the church seems to have cliques
    where people love darkness rather than light.

Come, my friends, you know such times;
    some days are soaked with gloom.
But shall we submit to life's shadows?
    Shall we add to life's sorrows?
When darkness appears to reign,
    that is the time to trust light.
When ugliness flaunts itself,
    then is the moment for beauty.
If life snarls up in meaninglessness,
    there is space for Christ's purposefulness.
When our path is stained with the suffering of man,
    then shall we recognize Christ's presence.

My friends, have we made our moods into an idol?
  Shall we obey our feelings rather than God?
Hey, everyone! Make a stand with me!
  Defy your feelings and trust the Lord!
Call the bluff of cloudy chaos
  and make room for some life and shape;
In the midst of gloom, God speaks,
  Saying, 'Let there be light'.

Healing

Psalm 51

In your dependable love, Lord, I find healing;
  your unconditional acceptance removes my shame.
I want to be washed clean,
  to be made like new again.
Excuses for my sins are no good;
  my failure to love stands out a mile.
Worst of all, my lovelessness hurts you;
  what I fail to do for others adds to your pain.
When I think of you suffering,
  I quite justly feel most miserable.
But you don't hold it against me;
  you help me recover from my shame.
Lord, I want to be remade deep down;
  the current of life in me needs transforming.
Lord, my feelings need purifying;
  my attitudes and ideas must be reshaped.
Above all things, Lord, don't ever leave me;
  nor remove your saving Spirit from me.
Help me to delight in you more than anything else;
  in the liberty you give, may I stand up straight.

His Arms

Lord, your arms reached out
  to save a vagrant world:
  baby arms, embracing mother and father;
  boyish hands, holding a sacred scroll;
  brotherly arms, helping family and friends.

Lord, your arms reached out
  to signal a new beginning:
  acknowledging the Baptist at the Jordan,
  beckoning to fishermen by the sea,
  pointing to the narrow way that leads to life.

Lord, your arms reached out
  to stop the pain around you:
  straightening curved spine and crippled leg,
  opening the eyes of the blind,
  touching the skin of the lonely leper.

Lord, your arms reached out
  to welcome those who despised themselves:
  sharing bread with outcasts,
  writing in the dust for a broken woman,
  shaking the hand of Zacchaeus.

Lord, your arms reached out
  to express the divine anger:
  pushing Peter out of your way,
  shaking a fist at arrogant Pharisees,
  cleansing the temple with a whip.

Lord, your arms reached out
  to bear the burden of man's sin:
  washing the feet of fickle disciples,
  carrying a cross through jeering crowds,
  embracing the world with crucified arms.

Lord, your arms reached out
   to break the bonds of awful death:
   greeting the astounded disciples,
   showing Thomas the wounds of love,
   sending your witnesses to the ends of the earth.

Lord, your arms reach out
   transcending time and space:
   beckoning us to turn and follow,
   serving us the bread and wine,
   touching us with renewing grace.

Lord, your hands shall reach out
   gathering folk from every nation:
   breaking down walls that divide us,
   reconciling humanity through your cross,
   handing to the Father the finished new creation!

Our Work

Lord, our attitude to work changes with our moods;
  we are as variable as the weather.
Some days we enjoy every moment of our work;
  other days we feel tired and resentful of it.
There are mornings when we dread the thought of getting up;
  but there are also times when we go to work gladly.

Lord, some of us get paid for doing the things we enjoy;
  others must work at distasteful tasks for their living.
Some of us work with kind and interesting people;
  others must work with sour and ugly characters.
Some who long for company must work alone;
  others who yearn for privacy must work with a crowd.

Sheepshearing, New South Wales.

Lord, whether we work for love or pleasure,
or whether it is only for duty or money,
We thank you for the privilege of daily work,
for the rewards of labour in whatever form.
In a world where millions are unemployed,
we count ourselves as richly blessed.

As products of the work of a loving Creator,
we thank you for skills of eye, brain, and hand.
As friends of the carpenter's Son of Nazareth,
we offer to you our work as an act of praise.
As children of the Spirit who has never ceased to work,
we seek to honour you in everything we do.

Happy People

Psalm 128

Happy are those who honour God,
sharing his ways.
You will work and eat;
fun and goodness will be yours.
Wife and husband, like fruitful trees,
shall tap the intimate joys of home.
Your children shall be like sturdy seedlings,
growing straight and tall.
That's how it will happen
for those who honour God!
Happiness will come from his Church,
and your worship will be a delight.
All the days of your life
you will delight in his growing family.
Peace be to God's people!
Peace be to his Church!

The Body
1 Corinthians 12

We are the Body of Christ,
    each one of us a limb or organ.
Let us glorify God in the use of our bodies,
    which is a most reasonable worship.

All who are Christ's hands —
    gifted in healing or helping,
    making music or machinery,
    painting, polishing or planting:
glorify God in your bodies.

All who are Christ's eyes —
    studying society and the Scriptures,
    noticing newcomer and nonentity,
    at microscopes, murals, and mathematics:
glorify God in your bodies.

All who are Christ's ears —
    aware of weeping and wandering,
    hearing harmony and hypocrisy,
    listening to laughter, logic and the lonely:
glorify God in your bodies.

You who are Christ's lips —
    teaching, training, testifying,
    singing, selling, satirizing,
    encouraging, enlightening, engendering:
glorify God in your bodies.

You who are Christ's feet —
    walking, working, waiting,
    striding into service and sacrifice,
    running to receive a prodigal:
glorify God in your bodies.

You who are Christ's heart —
  feeling the fellowship of faith,
  agonizing with Aboriginal and alcoholic,
  loving the least and the last:
glorify God in your bodies.

If one suffers, we all suffer;
  if one flourishes, we all rejoice.
We are the Body of Christ;
  let us glorify God in this holy Body.

Brother

Poor restless son
  of a tired mother-land,
wanders the gutters,
and — shaken — stutters,
  craving a brother's hand.

Pleads this son
  of an apathetic mother;
  patronized by his brother
with a one-dollar conscience,
or the supercilious nonsense
  of a pair of old boots
  and moth-wise suits.

Alone this brother
  waits in the park;
papers restless in the dusk-wind's sighing
chorus an infinite anguished crying,
  which the coming dark
  can't smother.

God's Strength
Psalm 121

When I gaze at the ancient mountains,
　　their huge strength steadies my trembling.
The strength of the Lord made the galaxies,
　　and shaped this dear old planet.
You can never stumble out of his care;
　　he who loves you never falls asleep.
The One who looks after you is awake,
　　always alert to the cries of his children.
Your God cares for you,
　　closer than your own right hand.
Even the fiery sun will not harm you,
　　nor the barren face of the moon.
God will keep you going in hard times;
　　he'll treasure your very being.
When you leave for work in the morning,
　　and when you return home at evening,
He will surely be with you,
　　this day and for ever.

The Nut, Stanley, Tasmania.

When

Lord, when my prayers are like a gibber plain,
and my soul like spinifex —
drench me with a downpour of mercy!

When I take things for granted
and gratitude goes to sleep —
put a new song on my tongue
till I praise as naturally as the bellbird.

When life's abrasive pressures fray me,
loosening my hold on the Still Centre —
tell me again about sparrows and magpies,
about wild lilies and pink heath,
and the Father who knows my needs.

When my miserly soul begrudges love,
complaining about importunate people,
or hides smugly in the folds of apathy —
put into my hands a crown of thorns,
and show me again what love can make
with two pieces of wood and a few nails.

Wave Rock, near Hyden, Western Australia.

This Mystery

There is a mystery
   wherein there is no confusion.
It is truth,
   which is never devised.
It is righteousness
   antecedent to every good deed.
It is justice, immeasurably larger
   than the righting of wrongs.
It is the beginning
   which is the end.
It is the weakness
   which is the only power.
It is the search
   which follows the finding.

The mystery is beneath the dignity
   of rulers, businessmen, and scientists,
Yet it is the origin
   of every beautiful deed
   which has ever enhanced the dignity of man.
It is the simplest idea,
   the most natural of deeds.

The fools of the world
   do not recognize this mystery
   even though they see its embodiment.
They do not follow the music,
   even though it surpasses all harmony.
They refuse to take it home
   because it cannot be bought.
They die without its joy
   because it's not the image of themselves.

The mystery dwells in you,
   and you in it.
Only when you love your own being
   can you know its truth.
And only when you trust its truth
   can you love your own being.

Here is the paradox
    which evades mere mind —
    but which envelops the whole being,
    inducting it into grace, mercy, and peace.

It confounds the philosophizers
    and scandalizes the religious.
It reveals itself
    in the deeds of a condemned rabbi,
    despised and rejected of men,
    a man of sorrows
    and acquainted with grief.

Judgment
Psalm 50

The only God has spoken;
  the Lord gives his word.
From beyond sunrise and sunset
  he calls the world to judgment;
From his city shines penetrating light,
  the radiance of sheer perfection.
Certainly he is coming,
  certainly he won't be silenced.
The fire of his presence will melt excuses;
  the wind of his spirit will break our defences.
Heaven and earth shall be summoned
  to the inescapable hour of reckoning.
Even his faithful friends must come,
  and the people of his covenant.
The skies shall ring with judgment
  when God delivers his verdict.

God's word is plain for the hypocrite;
  his grounds are completely clear:
'How dare you quote texts,
  you who evade renewal!
How can you glibly mouth my words,
  you who turn your backs?
You approve society's lawful thieves;
  you share in love's devaluation.
You are stuffed to the teeth with evil;
  your tongue frames smooth lies.
Every day you hound your brothers
  and stab your sisters in the back.
This and far worse you have done.
  Should I now keep quiet?
You even try to mould me in your own image!
  Openly shall I discipline you!'

Think about it,
  you who forget your God.
If the Lord tears your defences to pieces,
  who is there to save you?

But those who gladly give him all
   shall know a glorious freedom!
Those who worship in word and deed
   will see the salvation of God!

Dependable Word

Psalm 12

Help, Lord. What can we trust?
   Where is a dependable word?
Words no longer give communication,
   but are tuned for exploitation.
Men look us in the eye and lie;
   with secret motives they flatter us.
Lord, shut the lips of confidence men,
   and the tongues that exploit our pride.
Silence all media that twist the truth,
   the ad-men who can sell us destruction.

Listen! The Lord speaks,
   the only reliable voice is heard:
'Because of the plunder of the poor,
   and the groans of the lost,
I am among you, my people;
   I will protect you from the arrogant'.

This is the word we can trust,
   the pure word of Immanuel.
Like sterling silver is his word,
   refined seven times over.
He alone keeps his word,
   and saves us from the words around us.
Though scheming men oppose us,
   though voices cajole or bully us,
His word is the only word of life,
   the Word that endures for ever.

God Hidden and Present
Isaiah 63, 64

Lord, look from the place of your holiness,
   see us from the heights of your glory!
Where is your inspiration and courage?
   Your inflaming, caring love?
The saints and prophets cannot see us,
   Augustine and Luther cannot help us.
But you, Lord, are our Father,
   our kinsman from of old.
Why do you allow us to lose our way?
   Why let us become hard and godless?
For your servants' sake, do something!
   We are your own family!
Why permit despisers to stamp on our church?
   Why let them trample over sacred things?
We are treated as though outside your rule,
   like those who never received your call.

Why not leave your hiding and come among us,
   till the mountains quake in your presence!
Come, blazing like a forest fire,
   and bubbling like boiling water.
That would make unbelievers know you;
   the nations would tremble at your presence.
You have done unexpected things before,
   when the mountains shook at your coming.

We have indeed rebelled, and you have disciplined us,
   yet we continue on evil ways.
We have all become corrupted;
   even our goodness is as dirty rags.
We wither like old leaves;
   like the wind our sins sweep us away.
Nobody calls your name with total love,
   or clings to you in complete trust.
So you hide your presence from us,
   and allow our sins to consume us.

Today, Lord, we are as clay;
    you are the Master Potter.
We are your handiwork;
    you are our dear Father.

Ear has never heard,
    nor eye ever seen,
Any other god coming to the aid
    of those who patiently wait for him!
You welcome those who rejoice in goodness,
    and meet with those who remember your ways!

Hunger and Thirst

Unfathomable God,
you have given us hunger —
and the food to satisfy us,
the experience of thirst —
and the drink to quench it.
Can it be that,
hungering and thirsting for you,
we shall be denied satisfaction?

Water of life and Bread of heaven,
give us stubbornness in our seeking,
persistence in our partaking,
honesty in our questioning,
so that we may not despair
nor abandon the effort to pray;
not chase attractive substitutes,
nor fail to listen
to your witnesses.

Help us to creatively meditate
on the wisdom of Scripture —
the ugliness of human sin
and the sadness of death,
the wonder of divine love
and the life of Christ —
until our inner lives expand
and we begin to understand.

O loving God,
the beyond who is among us,
the thirst and the quenching,
the hunger and the satisfaction,
help us to live out our own prayers,
trusting you more lovingly,
listening more carefully,
and obeying more faithfully.

Then will our thirsty desert
blossom like a rose;
in our wilderness
we will eat manna;
in our seeking
we shall be surely found.
The glory of the Lord shall possess us,
the splendour of our God be revealed,
and we shall truly rest.

Sunrise, Moralana Scenic Drive, South Australia.

Forsaken?

My God! My God, why have you forsaken us —
forsaken us in the cry of the crucified!
In nis horrible helplessness
we are doubly helpless,
suffering by the million
and dying
alone.

My God! The nails that pierced Jesus cruelly,
surely pierce our one humanity;
the taunts from bystanders are ours:
the secret doubt that all
ends in an empty whimper,
bereft of light and
love.

My God! That his life should thus mercilessly end,
surrounded by such malignant rejection,
loved only by a frightened few
watching in fear,
leaves us all in
dereliction and
despair.

My God! Into that cold stone tomb
fall all our noblest human dreams;
the idealism of youth sinks
low in the deep shadows,
and even desperate defiance
in the darkness
weeps.

Dear God! On that black Friday you did not forsake us!
Not Jesus, nor any other desolate child of man!
That day you entered all our forsakenness,
tasting bitter dereliction and death,
shaping the valley of the shadow
to become an avenue of
hope.

We praise you, O God! We acknowledge you to be the Lord!
Despised and rejected, man of sorrows and grief,
great and marvellous are your deeds!
Wounded for our transgressions,
bruised for our iniquities,
God is with us!
Hallelujah!

Sweet and Sour

In this mysterious union of energy
   which we call humanity,
The black and the gold
   are so closely woven
That one cannot remove the pain
   without undoing the joy.

The gentle Buddhist,
   discovering this truth,
Removes both black and gold
   from his daily experience,
And calls the unsweetened, unbittered vestige
   the only peace.

Not so our Jesus,
   who embraces both
   with strong bleeding arms,
Affirming both Creator and creation
   as lovable —
And salvation as intrinsic
   to both the broken body and the shed blood,
   and the joy of wedding celebrations.

In this sweet and sour
   we spend our days.
In the unfolding of his purposes
We find our Lord giving the breath of life,
   while always
   his tears soak us,
   his joy uplifts us,
   and his love fills us.

PART III
These Are the Days

Advent 1

Come, Lord Jesus

'Come, Lord Jesus.'
'Come!' say the Spirit and the Church.
'Come!' let each hearer reply.
This same Jesus,
whom we love but no longer see,
shall come again in glory
to judge the living and the dead.
    Come, Lord Jesus.

Unexpected as a thief,
unexpected as a midnight guest,
unexpected as the lightning:
    Even so come, Lord Jesus.

To expose the hidden guilt,
to expose the schemes of men,
to expose the powers of darkness:
    Even so come, Lord Jesus.

Bringing judgment to the arrogant,
bringing discipline to the unfaithful,
bringing rebuke to the apathetic:
    Even so come, Lord Jesus.

Giving rest to the weary,
giving healing to the sick,
giving forgiveness to the repentant:
    Even so come, Lord Jesus.

Like light in darkness,
like water for the thirsty,
like a bridegroom for a bride:
    Even so come, Lord Jesus.

As the stiller of storms,
as the giver of living bread,
as the friend of sinners:
    Even so come, Lord Jesus.

With a kingdom for the poor,
with a world for the meek,
with rejoicing for the persecuted:
    Even so come, Lord Jesus.

Fulfilling the prayers of martyrs,
fulfilling the work of the cross,
fulfilling the resurrection joy:
    Even so come, Lord Jesus.

Mallacoota Beach, Victoria.

Advent 2

The Word within the Word

Most wonderful God, this is your world,
the fruit of your creating and redeeming word;
the word which shaped the history
out of which the Bible was written.

> For the Word from the beginning
> speaking as One who has authority,
> word of life:
> we thank you, Lord most high!

You spoke through many writers —
some simple and some sophisticated,
poets, historians, shepherds, and princes —
each inspired to pass the word on.

> For the Word which is a lamp,
> guide to our feet, beacon on our path,
> word of light:
> we thank you, Lord most high!

The scribes of many generations who toiled,
patiently reproducing the sacred scrolls,
you nurtured, God of the ages.
Through them your treasure came down to us.

> For those who delighted in your Word
> and forgot not your laws,
> word of truth:
> we thank you, Lord most high.

Translators you gave us, servants of the Word,
conveying the Good News in our native tongue;
Bede, Wycliffe, and the sages of King James,
Moffatt, Phillips, and scholars of today.

> For the Word that cannot be bound,
> skilfully spoken in due season,
> word like fire:
> we thank you, Lord most high.

You have given our nation your Word;
in Australia the Scriptures abound.
You have provided bookshops and Bible Societies,
and given us the freedom to share it.

For the Word that dwells richly in us,
and that never returns empty,
word that brings faith:
we thank you, Lord most high.

Wonderful God, we rejoice in the Gospel,
the witness of the Bible to Jesus Christ,
the Word within the words,
speaking a saving word to all people.

For the Word made flesh,
glorious Word who dwells among us,
word of love:
we praise you, Lord most high.

Advent 3

Prepare the Way of the Lord

There is a voice that cries in the wilderness,
the prophet word demanding change:
'Prepare the way of the Lord;
fill in the gullies, level the ridges,
straighten the crooked, move the mountains.
God's glory shall be revealed
and every eye shall see it.'

    Smooth the rough places,
    move the mountains;
    let God's glory be displayed!

In the wilderness of our cities,
furrowed by freeways and shaded by skyscrapers,
where hollow people jostle without love
or get lost in the wastes of suburbia,
where anonymous persons hide in flats,
or broken men queue up at hostels
for a bed and respite from dereliction:
Prepare the way of the Lord.

    Smooth the rough places,
    move the mountains;
    let God's glory be displayed!

In the wilderness of our countryside,
where little farmers eke out existence
while the rich accumulate massive farms
and city people play games on farmlets,
where once-proud towns shrink into shabbiness,
their sons and daughters drained off to the cities,
and unemployed blacks drink behind pubs:
Prepare the way of the Lord.

    Smooth the rough places,
    move the mountains;
    let God's glory be displayed!

In the wilderness of our schools and colleges,
the training-ground for survival of the fittest,
where the young learn almost everything
except how to become children of God,
expanding in mind but not in soul;
where young people earn diplomas, but little wisdom,
or graduate with honours in all but love:
Prepare the way of the Lord.

    Smooth the rough places,
    move the mountains;
    let God's glory be displayed!

In the wilderness of our politics,
a field of stones and shabby fame,
where some blatantly offer election bribes
or have the gall to say they're the greatest,
where caring members can get mauled by power-brokers
and are relegated to the back benches
till cynicism breeds like a horrible virus:
Prepare the way of the Lord.

    Smooth the rough places,
    move the mountains;
    let God's glory be displayed!

In the wilderness of our religions
where theological fashions come and go,
buildings and crowds persist as status-symbols,
and pomp and circumstance are high on the ratings,
where evangelism can be considered poor taste,
prayer and sacrifice as optional extras,
and even Jesus is feared as 'extremist':
Prepare the way of the Lord.

    Smooth the rough places,
    move the mountains;
    let God's glory be displayed!

Voice in the wilderness, what shall we do?
Prophet of the Lord, what is the word?
'Turn, turn, turn to the Lord;
you who have two suits, give to the naked;
if you eat well, share with the hungry;
in business and authority, deal with compassion —
and be ready for the One who comes with fire.'

    Smooth the rough places,
    move the mountains;
    let God's glory be displayed!

Nullarbor Highway, South Australia.

Advent 4

He Comes
Psalm 24

He comes to his own world,
   though his own will not receive him.
Everything already belongs to him
   and the people of every nation.
From sea to sea he created it;
   all living things are his joy.

Can any of us dare face him?
   Or keep our poise in his presence?
If our hands had never harmed another,
   if our motives were perfectly pure,
If we had never been seduced by vanity,
   if no trace of deceit lingered in us,
Then we would boldly receive him,
   confidently seeking his blessing.

Corrupt we all are, yet we seek him;
   our generation searches for a god.
We are creatures who are always restless,
   seeking elusive security and peace.
We look for his face in our heroes;
   vainly we search in our libraries.

Lift up your tired heads!
   Open up your weary eyes!
The King of glory comes among us;
   he enters the gates of our humanity.
Who is this King of glory?
   The Lord who stoops to conquer,
The Lord of Shepherds and poor men,
   he is the King of glory!

Lift up your tired heads!
   Open your weary eyes!
The King of glory comes to you.
   Who is this King of glory?
The Lord of countless hosts,
   he is our King of glory!

The Leap Forward

Lord, shall Christmas come again
distracting us momentarily
from the boasts and myths
of that Babel we call civilization,
giving us a few days playing
at worshipping the Mystery —
before we rush back
to the world of contemporary fantasy
where diseased minds pretend
the real action is?

Lord, the things we laud as progress,
and name as giant steps forward,
are only the fancy footwork
of those who dance on the same spot,
dazzling the eyes that look on
with smart improvisations —
until we fail to see
how little we step forward
and how rarely we leap.

Lord, yours is the only advance.
That potent Bethlehem gift
is a tiny, weak thing
unable to walk, stand, or even sit —
yet in the hour of birth
leaping forward over ages,
and inviting us to follow
in this new and holy way
where even our few steps forward
release joy among herald angels.

Lord, now dawns our day of progress!
*Little son of God, laid in a manger,
we adore your coming!
Now God is our image, of our flesh and blood!
You are our Saviour and brother
who lies in a cot.
You lie in our misery,
share all our needs,
and assure us of glory!
Hallelujah!

* Thoughts from Martin Luther.

On Christmas Eve

Glory to God in the highest,
    and on earth peace, goodwill toward men!

The dry grass has turned light brown,
    crackling under footsteps like crisp paper.
Soak-hoses and sprinklers are at work,
    greening gardens and preserving shrubs.
The starlings arrive for a drink,
    while two brown doves take a shower.
In the old palm trees the sparrows gossip,
    and from the gum trees cicadas sing.

The highways are already thick with cars,
    packed with parents, presents, children, and pets.
In city parks crowds gather at dusk
    to sing by candlelight the much-loved carols.
Near midnight many stream into churches,
    ordinary people sharing an extraordinary faith:
Glorifying again the Word made flesh,
    tasting the royal Bread and priceless Wine.

Tomorrow the summer sun will wake us early,
    the few hours' sleep swiftly fled.
Even then, children will be out on the footpaths,
    their scooters, prams, and bikes sparkling.
At church, family worship will have many guests —
    cousins, grandparents, new toy bears, and dolls!
Outside church, more cards, kisses, and greetings —
    'Merry Christmas' under the hot morning sun.

By midday the aroma of turkey and mint peas
    will blend with the fragrance of fruit salad and puddings;
The scent of pollens on a warm summer wind,
    mixed with the smell of pine needles and fruit punch.
Chatter, eating, and laughter — all blending
    with fond memories of other years:
The personal, spiritual, and secular
    poured together into one incarnational celebration.

It's Christmas Eve again in this lucky country;
    Christ's birthday awaited under evening skies.
Dear God, what a holy day tomorrow will be!
    What a celebration of life and love!

With the whole church on earth and in heaven,
    we join in the angels' song:
'Glory to God in the highest,
    and on earth peace, goodwill toward men'.

Christmas

Rejoice, Australia, in God your Saviour!
　Celebrate today the Christmas Gift.
From Launceston, Broome, Cairns, and Mt Gambier,
　let the story be told and the carols uplift.
In the hot dusty inland, sing his glad music;
　on crowded beaches, remember his birth.
Christ Jesus has come among us for ever;
　his birthday offers a new hope on earth.

Let mountain ash, karri, and blackwood salute him.
　jacaranda, banksia, fern, and flame tree.
Let dry places blossom with blue cattle bushes,
　and plains turn red with Sturt desert pea.
Rejoice, you mountains, bushland, and forest;
　heath and waratah make gay jubilee!

Run like the wind, long-legged emu,
　to all remote creatures carry the word!
Leap for joy, wallaby, kangaroo, and quokka;
　dance, elegant brolga and shy lyre bird!
Chatter the story, bright lorikeets and parrots,
　give all flying things the news you have heard!

Join the celebration, all human population —
　late arrivals to the great south land!
All families, come and worship in country and city,
　at inland homesteads, or on warm beach sand!
Black people, make him your best corroborees!
　Descendants of pioneers, sing your praise!
New Australians from Asia, Africa, and Europe,
　offer the heritage of your ancient ways!

Rejoice, Australia, in God your Saviour;
　exult, old continent and young nation!
In the arms of the Virgin, see your salvation,
　the destiny awaited for countless years.
Arise, and laugh, and dance, and sing,
　for the Antipodes, too, have a glorious King!

Your Day

Jesus, how strong
and irrepressible
is this your day.

Though hedged by greed
and masked by tinsel,
it has its say.

Our crowds disperse
and turn tired eyes
to where you lay.

Some spurn the sign.
Rapt, others find God
in human clay!

For the New Year

Sing to the Lord a New Year's song!
Give him the highest New Year honours:
   Thank the Lord for the old year ended,
   Trust him at the dawning of the new.
   Lift our faces to the midnight sky and rejoice!
   Let the Southern Cross be our pilgrim sign.

Praise the Lord for the things that endure;
Old things transcending the changing years:
   The solid soil of our ancient land under our feet;
   Incessant seas that wash our shores from Hobart to Darwin;
   The morning sun rising on a familiar landscape;
   The westerlies spinning windmills or dispersing city smog;
   After rains, the dry Centre blossoming in profusion;
   Trees on the Great Divide reaching tall for the sky;
   Your divine purpose brooding over Australia,
   Loving our land long before we shared it;
   Your divine mercy encircling every person,
   Speaking our names in a hundred different accents.
   Among us the saving deeds of Jesus Christ —
   The same yesterday, today, and for ever!

Praise the Lord for new possibilities being born,
New lights that gleam on every horizon:
   The strengthening of faith and enlarging of vision;
   The fellowship of Christ in success or failure;
   Readiness to care for needy fellow-citizens —
   The physically, socially, or spiritually handicapped;
   Liberation from political and religious prejudice,
   And a hearty commitment to the ways of Jesus;
   The willingness to listen to the words of an opponent;
   The courage to speak up when cowards become dumb;
   The chance to break idols of possessions and position;
   Worshipping the power that is made perfect in weakness;
   Discarding personal day-dreams for the dreams of our Lord —
   The same yesterday, today, and for ever!

Sing to the Lord a New Year's song!
Give him the choicest of New Year honours:
    As we greet one another with 'Happy New Year',
    Greet him as the Lord of every minute.
    For his call will be renewed each morning,
    And his peace shall be ours at close of every day.

Epiphany

Arise, Australia, arise,
    for your light has surely come!
The glory of the Lord is risen upon you,
    and the darkness cannot quench it.
We, too, have seen the rising of his star,
    and have come to worship him.
Jesus, light of the world, we honour you!
    Jesus, light in our national darkness, we need you!

Come, Prime Minister and Premier, stand in his light;
    parliaments and councils, learn his ways.
Come, business and trade unions, stand in his light;
    managers and shop stewards, hear his good news.

Let Sydney and Melbourne respond to his rising,
    Canberra and Darwin his freedom receive.
Let Perth and Hobart respond to his rising,
    Adelaide and Brisbane discover his love.

Turn, magistrate and judge, face his glory;
    lawyers and jurors, discover his laws.
Turn, teacher and professor, face his glory;
    graduates and students, give him your lives.

Let Port Hedland and Port Arthur respond to his rising,
    Gundagai and Coober Pedy receive his rare joy.
Let Broken Hill and Mt Isa respond to his rising,
    Goondiwindi and Dimboola share his new day!

Journey, farmer and grazier, to follow his star;
    shearers and stockmen, venture a prayer.
Journey, miner and timberman, to follow his star;
    powder-monkey and truckies, acquire his power.

Arise, Australia, arise and sing,
  your light has surely come!
The light and glory of a holy God
  in the face of Bethlehem's Son.
We, too, have seen the rising of his star,
  and have come to worship him.
O that men would praise the Lord for his goodness,
  and his wonderful works to the children of men!

Senator Neville Bonner.

Lent 1

The Way of the Cross

If anyone wants to come with me, he must forget self,
take up his cross every day, and follow me. Luke 9:23 (TEV)

Lord, this is a troublesome saying,
    heavy and hard.
We jealously protect our gains,
    always on guard.
The more we have the more we crave,
    success self-made.
When you speak of losing all,
    we are afraid.

Lord, this is an embarrassing saying
    for folk like us.
Even over the smallest disciplines
    we make a great fuss.
We are not made of the stuff of heroes,
    without complaints.
We are just your little people,
    not noble saints.

Lord, this is a persistent saying,
    giving no rest.
In mind and soul we know it is sane,
    offering the best.
By gaining and grasping we know we lose
    life's deeper scope.
The strange logic of your cross remains
    life's only hope.

Lord, this is a saving saying,
    divine outlay.
The path of the cross the only glory
    all the way.
Willing, though fearful, help us to bear it,
    not growing slack.
Laughing and crying, help us to follow,
    not turning back.

Following in His Ways
Psalm 25

Our Lord, on you I rest my very being;
    on you I stake my life.
Don't let me ever be ashamed,
    or discouraged by the success of opponents.
No person who follows you is disgraced —
    only those who are unfaithful.

Show me, Lord, the disciple's path;
    teach me your ways.
Saviour, lead me and coach me;
    every day I'll trust your saving love.
Remember your unfailing compassion,
    shown throughout the ages.

Recall not the faults of my youth;
    remember me in your saving grace.
You alone are good and true;
    therefore show wanderers the way to go.
You guide ordinary folk aright;
    you teach the timid your way.

Lord, your loving ways are sure
    to those who follow and obey.
Your purpose is shown to true worshippers,
    and we experience your covenant.
I keep my eyes on you always;
    only you can save my feet from trouble.

When I feel lonely or depressed,
    Lord, turn back and encourage me.
If I grieve within my heart,
    free me from my distress.
When you see my anxiety and doubt,
    forgive my every sin.

Lent 2

Not by Bread Alone

Man cannot live on bread alone, but needs every
word that God speaks. Matthew 4:4 (TEV)

I do have faith, but not enough. Help me to have more.
Mark 9:24 (TEV)

In a world where people live for pride,
eating the bread of vanity:
from the conceit that looks for public
    praise and honours;
from the vainglory that flaunts diplomas
    and degrees;
from the arrogance of religious and
    moral swagger;
from the insolence of supposed racial
    superiority,
save your children, Lord.

In a world where people live by force,
eating the bread of power:
from all attempts to manipulate
    our friends;
from the temptation to scorn a
    defeated opponent;
from the desire to use chance advantages
    to disadvantage others;
from leaders who love to rule
    more than to serve,
save your children, Lord.

In a world where people live by greed,
eating the bread of cupidity:
from envy of those
    with larger homes;
from selling our ethics
    for a few more dollars;

from trusting the stock-market
   more than the Scriptures;
from supporting only those charities
   which offer an income tax deduction,
save your children, Lord.

In a world where people live by pleasure,
eating the bread of sensuality:
from turning food
   into an extravagant habit;
from cluttering our homes
   with technological toys;
from using our sexuality
   for indulgent lust;
from loving things
   and using people,
save your children, Lord.

Sydney Domain

For the Affluent
Psalm 49

Hear this, all Australians!
   Listen, all people on earth,
The teeming millions and every single person,
   the affluent and the needy!
For I have a sane word to speak,
   the truth from a full heart.

There are many who trust money,
   and show off their wealth.
Yet none can ransom themselves,
   nor bribe God for redemption.
To ransom their soul is far too costly,
   for ever beyond their means.

Remember: even smart people die;
   so, too, do the foolish and the callous.
All wealth is left for others;
   our home becomes the grave —
the place where we must remain
   though our name might linger on a business.

The privileged have no exemption;
   like animals we all perish.
Such is the destiny of fools,
   and of all who admire them.
Like sheep they flock to doom,
   with death their only shepherd.

Do not stand in awe of a rich man,
   who lives in an extravagant home.
He can take nothing with him when he dies;
   his vainglory shall not follow him.
But God shall ransom his humble people;
   he shall save us from the power of death.

Lent 3

Don't Tempt God

Psalm 82

God takes a stand in the council of heaven,
  to judge those who live like gods.

How long will you encourage injustice,
  and give benefits to evil men?
You should lift up the weak and the orphan,
  give rights to all downtrodden people.
You should rescue the weak and the poor,
  freeing them from the grip of exploiters.
But you do not want to know,
  you are not willing to understand;
You stroll in the darkness
  while the foundation of the world shakes!

I tell you, though you could be godlike,
  children of the Most High,
You shall soon die like all men,
  you shall fall like all proud men.

O God, take your stand and judge us!
  The nations are at your disposal!

Don't Test God

The scripture also says, 'Do not put the Lord your God to the test'. Matthew 4:7 (TEV)

You must not test the Lord your God,
   nor ask for a sign of his presence;
His commandments are already given,
   guide-posts on the road to life.
His sign is imbedded in our history,
   the child of a young woman — Immanuel.
Only a wicked and perverse generation
   dare seek a greater sign than this.

Christ-given signs of his presence are with us:
   the haunted eyes of the starving
   looking at the camera of the tourist,
   and the pitiful band of refugees
   through whom Christ cries to us.
   As we sit at plenteous tables,
   or sleep in secure comfort,
   should we ask for other signs?
   Dare we test the Lord our God?

His signs are in our hospitals:
   thousands of road-accident victims,
   some dying, but not quickly enough,
   and many with no future
   except wheelchairs, callipers, or mindless years.
   Dare we test the Lord our God
   by saying prayers
   and then driving carelessly
   on our streets and highways?

The signs are in our churches:
  ordinary people with simple faith
  who humbly extend themselves
  with an extraordinary compassion
  in a thousand little actions;
  the unpretentious, grass-roots love
  which asks for no reward.
  Dare we test the Lord our God
  by demanding signs more grand?

Precious signs are in the Supper:
  fruits of our toil and the generosity of God;
  where the grace of soil, rain, and sunshine
  condense in a chalice
  and a piece of daily bread;
  where people meet with an everloving Host.
  Dare we test the Lord our God
  by asking for signs more profound?

Lent 4

One Lord
Psalm 33

If you are joyful, show it to the Lord!
    Stand tall and praise him!
Let music tell your gratitude:
    organ and guitar, trumpet and drums.
Haven't you a new song to sing?
    Put your whole strength into it.

What the Lord tells you is true;
    whatever he does is dependable.
He has a passion for integrity and justice,
    and sufficient love to fill the world.
Happy our nation when the Lord is God,
    when our people respond to his call.

The universe was framed from his words;
    the galaxies are his thoughts.
All the oceans are his waterbag,
    the Indian and Tasman his finger-bowl.
Let everything tremble before the Lord,
    every person stand in awe!

He scatters the diplomacy of empires;
    the Lord foils the schemes of the cunning.
Nations are not saved by vast armies,
    nor soldiers by brute strength.
Tanks and rockets don't give safety;
    no one wins by military power.

The purposes of the Lord are infinite;
    his plans extend from age to age.
Intimately he shapes the life of all,
    and broods over every single soul.
He is well aware of those who honour him;
    those who put all hope in his free grace.

Come, everyone! Let us place our hope in him!
  Let us love our helper and guardian.
Every fibre of our being rejoices in him,
  trusting his healing name.
Lord, let your sure love reside with us,
  for we have no hope or joy but you.

Crater Lake, Tasmania.

Lent 4

God Alone

*The scripture says, 'Worship the Lord your God
and serve only him!' Matthew 4:10 (TEV)*

Jesus, on your high mountain I paused;
    I paused, watched, and pondered.
Below were my countrymen
    scurrying from coast to coast
in a frenzy of activity,
    pouring out vast energy
in a fervent search for joy.

I saw them like hungry scavengers,
    tearing hills apart for iron or lead,
burrowing into mountains for copper and zinc,
    ransacking the countryside for bauxite and rutile;
and towns grew up and facilities flourished,
    bridges spanned chasms, and airports were levelled —
but rare were the signs of joy.

I saw them feverishly building their cities,
    shops, banks, supermarkets, and factories,
universities, schools, town halls, and skyscrapers,
    freeways, suburbs, ferries, and railways.
The traffic lights blinked and the hordes rushed,
    the motor cars reared and the neon signs flashed —
but rare were the sounds of joy.

I saw them at play in city and country,
    races at Flemington and 'pokies' at Paddington,
chasing leather footballs in three varieties,
    striding down fairways or riding the waves,
white-clad contestants at cricket, bowls, or tennis,
    and for every sportsman a thousand watching 'telly' —
yet rare were the songs of joy.

I saw them at politics, zealous and vehement,
    canvassing for votes and playing with power,
paying homage to position, policy, and 'party',
    dancing to the tune of the opinion polls.
Endless rumbling words, tactics and meetings,
    boasting and evading with no sign of shame —
but rare were the sessions of joy.

Lord, from your high mountain I saw my countrymen,
    my people whom I love and loathe,
whom I deeply trust but fear;
    their energy was surprising, their persistence impressive,
their homage to their gods was most sincere.
    Some wore emblems and some wore crosses —
but rare were the scenes of joy.

Lent 5

The Lost

*The Son of Man came to seek and to save
the lost.* Luke 19:10 (TEV)

Lord, we get lost so easily:
    in the course of conversation,
    at the house of a neighbour,
    with good advice on our lips,
we get lost in our wisdom
and lose the gift of truth.

Lord, we get lost so unexpectedly:
    in the hour of success,
    at the home of a friend,
    with hymns on our tongues,
we get lost in our importance
and lose the gift of joy.

Lord, we get lost so crudely:
    in the middle of our prayers,
    at the party or the club,
    with humour in our words,
we get lost in our adaptability
and lose the gift of peace.

Lord, we get lost so profoundly:
    in the cause of Christian duty,
    at the social justice meeting,
    or with consecrated bread in our hands,
we get lost in our righteousness
and lose the gift of love.

Lord, we are found so simply:
    in the moment of awareness,
    at the hour of taking stock,
    with hunger in our being,
we lose ourselves in grace
and find the gift of life.

From the Depths
Psalm 130

Out of deep anguish I cry to you, Lord;
  Lord, can you hear me?
To the groaning of my prayers
  please carefully listen.
If you, Lord, keep a record of sins,
  then none of us dare face you.
But in you we find forgiveness,
  therefore we can adore you.
I wait, with all my soul I wait,
  and hope for the word I need.
With all my soul I long for my Lord,
  more than night-watchmen waiting for dawn.
Like the weary looking for sunrise,
  let all God's people wait in hope.
For with the Lord there is pure love,
  with him is abundant liberty.
He alone can set us free
  from all our sins.

Lent 6

Hosanna

Zechariah 7 - 9

Sing and rejoice, daughters of God!
   Shout for joy, sons of the Father!
Here comes your King
   travelling to his victory;
Riding humbly on a donkey,
   on a foal not ridden before.
Hosanna! All joy to our King!
   To the one who comes in the name of the Lord!

But my countrymen will not cheer;
   my people grumble at his coming.
Though their idols are useless,
   and their heroes are deceivers,
Though they wander like lost sheep
   without a loving shepherd,
Yet they will not listen,
   nor obey the word of the Lord.

He speaks up for true justice:
   'Give loyalty and compassion;
Care for the orphan and the pensioner;
   aid the refugee and those in poverty;
Do not ruthlessly exploit,
   or plot trouble for each other'.
But people will not listen;
   they shrug their shoulders and prepare a cross.

Ride on in majesty, King of love;
   show us the way that leads to peace.
The Lord shall banish our armies;
   our armaments shall be destroyed.
He shall speak reconciliation to every nation,
   extending his love from sea to sea.
This Kingdom which seems impossible
   shall surely come to be.

Hosanna! Keep steady your hands!
  Hear the word of the Lord of hosts:
Love shall reign in the city of God,
  old people shall sit in its squares;
Its streets shall be filled with children
  playing without any fears.
The Lord will dwell with his people,
  and banish all sorrow and cares.

Palm Sunday service of worship and witness, Mt Waverley, Victoria, 1973.

Good Friday

Lord, truly you have borne our griefs
    and carried our sorrows.
On this most terrible and wonderful day,
    when the sun was dimmed
    and the earth shuddered in horror,
We know it.

Lord, no longer is it only the blood of our brother
    that cries out from the ground.
Today we hear the voice of the blood of God
    pleading from the soil
    with a claim which will never be silenced
Or ever defeated.

Lord, everywhere we go your holy blood speaks:
    from the rocky soil of Israel,
The green fields of Devon and the vineyards of the Rhine,
    out of the clays of Uganda,
    from the prairies of Canada and rice paddies of Vietnam:
The cry of love.

Lord, our homeland, too, shudders in loving recognition,
    everywhere is now Golgotha:
Yanchep and Wilpena, Gove, Burnie, and Kingaroy,
    sheep stations and dairy farms,
    Blue Mountains and Wimmera wheatlands, all cry with the blood
Of the crucified God.

Lord, if in love we offered you our homeland,
    it would be poor thanks;
If the whole wealth of Mother Earth were given,
    even that would be inadequate praise.
O you who bear our griefs and carry our sorrows,
We are yours!

Easter

Christ is risen!
   Christ is risen indeed!
Come, you States and territories, glorify the Lord!
   From coast to coast, tell of his love!
Today all our defeats are defeated,
   and death is swallowed up in victory!

Praise him, all you Aboriginal people,
   your humiliation is not for ever!
Praise him, all unwanted and unemployed people,
   your dejection shall be turned into joy!
Praise him, all prisoners in cells or in drug addiction,
   your liberation begins at the empty tomb!
Praise him, all despairing and cynical people,
   your fears are rolled away with the stone!
Praise him, all lonely and homesick migrants,
   your risen Lord walks Australian streets, too!
Praise him, all who hurt from fresh bereavements,
   your grief can be mingled with peace.
Praise him, all half-hearted Christians,
   your Lord makes all things new!

Christ is risen!
   He is risen indeed!
With angels and archangels, and all the company of heaven,
   let Australians glorify his holy name!
Today all our defeats are defeated,
   and death is swallowed up in victory!

Pentecost

Lord, you come
like the wind
and the earth grows
hale at your breath.
You brood
over the face of the waters,
and in the Body of the Church,
shaping
the world that is to be.

You arrive —
like the wind filling a thousand sails
on Sydney Harbour —
and fill
our slack churches
with new power
and vision.

Like moist air
carrying refreshing rain
to the Flinders Ranges,
clothing the valleys with red hops,
carpeting the slopes with purple and gold,
so your Spirit
brings the colour of Christ
into drab communities.

You sweep in,
fresh as sea breezes across Port Phillip
bringing relief and restoration
to a hot and tired city,
dispersing the smog,
encouraging us to breathe deeply again
of the Breath of life.

Sometimes you roar
like a hurricane,
tearing away
the flimsy structures
of our gaudy materialism,
demolishing us
to the Ground of our Being.

As strong as a summer wind
transporting a myriad of seeds
to impregnate distant plains
with new patterns of life,
so you seed us
with new faith,
fertile from the Teller of parables.

Warm as the breath
of a loved one
whispering forgiveness
and unearned respect,
so your Spirit
breathes renovating grace
into our dispirited souls.

Some days you spin
like a willy-willy,
startling, tearing, hurting,
uprooting us from apathy
and leaving us giddy
with new possibilities
in discipleship.

Like a soft breeze at dusk
soothing tired faces
at the end of a hard day,
so you visit us
in the evening of life
when all our work is done,
giving us Christ's peace at the last.

We believe
in the Holy Spirit,
Lord, and giver of life,
Poured out on all flesh,
Who with the Father
and the Son,
is worshipped and glorified!
Amen!

Life in the Spirit

When earth was like a valley of skeletons,
   you, wonderful God, came among us in power!
Your Jesus breathed on us and said:
   'Receive the Holy Spirit'.
Like a mighty rushing wind:
   'Receive the Holy Spirit'.
Like tongues of living fire:
   'Receive the Holy Spirit'.
With love to the whole world:
   'Receive the Holy Spirit'.

Lord, if we had not seen and heard,
   we would not believe it;
That this valley of dry bones should live
   is beyond our wildest expectations!
Yet now we hear rattling of bones
   as dead and forgotten hopes reassemble;
We witness the astounding omen
   of broken, impotent promises growing muscle;
Surprised, we watch old eye-sockets
   filling with new and loving visions;
Cold arms pulse as with new blood,
   embracing lonely and uncherished people;
Deadly-dull churchgoers stand tall
   and celebrate the Gospel with style.
We see atrophied hands and feet inspired
   to do the costly deeds of Jesus;
Bare bones, bleached by the winds of materialism,
   become enfleshed with faith and love;
We hear voices, long ago incapable of blessing,
   commence to sing the song of the angels.
Before our very eyes, unforgiving, bitter skeletons
   begin to be merciful, even as our Father is merciful;
Grey, defeated forms, who despaired of any joy,
   run and dance their way into the Kingdom!

Holy Spirit, Lord, and giver of life,
    praise belongs to you for ever!
The Gospel is announced to the poor:
    praise belongs to you for ever!
Release for prisoners, sight for the blind;
Yes, the time has come
    when the Lord will save his people:
    praise belongs to you for ever!

Our God

Your rainbow shines
    its hope across all lands:
Christ's new creation,
    grasped by loving hands.

You are the bridge
    which spans our separation;
Christ's life laid down
    the new foundation.

Your vast acceptance
    liberates from fear;
Christ's fellow-heirs
    high-spirited appear.

Full of surprises
    is Christ's God and ours;
the weak rejoice
    in unexpected powers.

Our roots grow deep,
    firm in the ground which holds us;
Christ's subtle strength
    where love enfolds us.

All Saints' Day
Psalm 94

Lord, you are a God of justice;
    show it to my countrymen!
Ruler of the whole cosmos,
    give the arrogant what they deserve!
How long is it going to go on, Lord —
    this insolence of heartless power-brokers?

Lord, it burns me up,
    the way weak people are exploited.
Aborigines have their sacred shrines despoiled,
    ravaged for mineral deposits.
Widows and migrants are sucked in,
    fooled by the fine print in hire-purchase agreements.
Grog and drugs are peddled to our youth,
    and they slaughter each other on the roads.

Yet, Lord, big business brags about it,
    publishing its profits in the financial pages.
Shareholders are sometimes demonic, Lord,
    when profits become the only value.
Ordinary people seem far removed,
    pawns without names or faces.
Our sophistical friends tell us not to worry;
    God doesn't care, so why should we?

Listen, you well-groomed dumb-heads!
    Suave fools, wake up to yourselves!
Does he who created ears hear no crying,
    the Lord who gave eyes see no suffering?
Can't he who instructs the nations give correction?
    Doesn't the teacher of mankind know anything?
The Lord knows our sophisticated minds;
    we are nothing but foul wind-bags!

Happiness is accepting the Lord's discipline,
  learning the ways of love;
Standing firm when all goes against you,
  until the wicked fall into their own pit.
The Lord will never abandon his people;
  he won't walk out on his own.
In the end, goodness will have its way;
  the future belongs to compassionate people.

Who will stand with me against apathy?
  Who sides with me against corruption?
If the Lord had not helped me,
  I would have been in the cemetery long ago!
When I find myself giving in,
  your love, Lord, holds me up.
When anxiety seizes my mind,
  your presence is my comfort and joy.

Lord, can corporate evil get your vote,
  or those who twist the law defeat us —
Those who slander good men as troublemakers
  and allow defenceless people to die?
No way! The Lord is utterly dependable;
  my God is more solid than granite.
In the Lord's own time they will fall;
  'respectable' crime will get what it deserves!

Australia Day
Psalm 136

Thank the Lord, the source of all goodness,
The True-God of True-God,
    His love endures for ever!
Thank the Ruler of all rulers,
Who alone achieves the impossible.
    His love endures for ever!

His wisdom made boundless galaxies,
He placed this planet in orbit,
And gave us lights to order our lives;
By day the sun, moon and stars by night.
    His love endures for ever!

Oppressors he has punished;
Pharaoh of old, and Hitler in our century.
His faithful people he has rescued:
Moses, Peter, Luther, Knox, and Niemoller.
    His love endures for ever!

He sailed with the convicts to Botany Bay,
Brought down unscrupulous governors,
Led settlers through alien bush,
And turned prisoners into free men.
    His love endures for ever!

He gave a homeland to unwanted people,
A rich heritage to those who serve him.
When we were under attack he remembered us,
Rescued us from those who sought to invade us.
    His love endures for ever!

Nor does the Lord forget his lowly creatures:
Platypus and pelican eat well.
He gives grass for the wallaroo and seeds for lorikeets;
He feeds the marsupial mouse and the echidna.
O give thanks to the God of every living thing!
    His love endures for ever!

Brisbane skyline.

Anzac Day

Psalm 90

Lord, the ages come and go,
    but you remain as our homing-point.
Before you gave birth to mountains,
    before the travail of this planet,
Back beyond the beginning,
    you have been God.

You return every person to dust,
    saying: 'Back you go, mortals'.
In your eyes a thousand years are like yesterday,
    or like an hour's sleep during the night.
You sweep people away like a flood;
    we are as grass in the early morning —
In the morning it bursts with green life,
    yet by evening it is cut and withered.
So are we consumed by your discipline,
    and by your power we are dismissed.
Our mistakes are naked before you,
    our guilty secrets are exposed to your glance.
Every day dissolves in your power;
    our life ends as suddenly as a short story.
We only live for about seventy years —
    if we are strong, perhaps eighty.
It is a span of struggle and grief;
    soon it is over and we take wing.
Yet do we make time to think of your discipline?
    And who gives respect equal to your power?

Please teach us to treasure every day,
    taking to heart your brand of wisdom.
Stand by us, Lord, through every long day;
    have pity on all your workers.
Fill us with your free love,
    so that we may laugh and sing.
Give us joy to match our daily grind,
    and happiness to mix with the years of pain.
Help your workers to see you at work among us,
    that our children may recognize your glory.
We want the beauty of our God to be upon us,
    till the works of our hands share your eternal purpose.

Church Anniversary

Enter these doors with thanksgiving,
   come into this sanctuary with praise;
Be grateful for the gift of the Church Universal,
   and praise the Lord for the church in this place.

For . . . years of continuous worship;
   for . . . years of sincere service;
     we thank you, O Lord.
For those who initiated this fellowship,
   and those who built this sanctuary:
     we thank you, O Lord.
For people who used their gifts of leadership,
   and people who gave loyalty and love:
     we thank you, O Lord.
For the Gospel proclaimed in this church,
   and the Gospel received within these walls:
     we thank you, O Lord.
For all who in sorrow found comfort,
   and all who in weakness found strength:
     we thank you, O Lord.
For the fellowship which has given support,
   and the fellowship which has challenged and disturbed:
     we thank you, O Lord.
For times when this church has been packed,
   and times when only a few have worshipped:
     we thank you, O Lord.
For the rich memories of years gone by,
   and the opportunities in years to come:
     we praise you, O Lord most High.

Your Church, O God, has embraced us;
   Its one loving Lord has redeemed us.
With all your people who ever were, are, or will be,
   we would worship and serve you for ever!

Come Quickly!
Psalm 63

My God in whom I trust,
    I look for your early coming.
Body and soul, I thirst for you
    like a man lost in the outback.
Through country and city I search for you,
    looking for signs of your glory.
Your love is dearer than life itself;
    my lips hunger for adequate praise.
As long as I live I'll serve you;
    my hands shall honour your name.

When you come I shall be satisfied,
    as a guest at a King's table.
I'll lie awake on my bed,
    marvelling at your hospitality.
For you are my only help;
    in your coming is true joy.
Willingly I'll be a disciple,
    your strong hand pointing the way.

The false goals that distract me
    shall crumble into the dust;
Everything that threatens my hope
    shall be as carrion for the crows.
All deceit shall be silenced
    when allegiance is sworn to you.
Let every ruler rejoice in you
    when you come to be our King!

Photo Credits

Page
11 Seals at Seal Bay, SA — Publicity and Design Services, Premier's Dpt, SA
15 Outback signposts — Dpt of Tourism, Qld
18 Fruitcart, Rundle Mall, Adelaide — Publicity and Design Services, Premier's Dpt, SA
22 Brushtailed possums — Dpt of Tourism, Qld
25 Wheatfields — WA Dpt of Tourism
30 Most s-w tip of Australia, Cape Leeuwin, WA — B.D. Prewer
35 Stand of wattles — WA Dpt of Tourism
41 Sydney Harbour and Opera House — Dpt of Tourism, NSW
45 Reflections, Wynyard Lake, Tas. — B.D. Prewer
52 Tanks and windmill — Dpt of Tourism, NSW
56 Ayers Rock — NT Tourist Board
62 Sheepshearing — Dpt of Tourism, NSW
66 The Nut, Stanley, Tas. — Dpt of Tourism, Tas.
67 Wave Rock, near Hyden, WA — WA Dpt of Tourism
75 Sunrise, Moralana Scenic Drive, SA — Publicity and Design Services, Premier's Dpt, SA
81 Mallacoota Beach, Vic. — B.D. Prewer
86 Nullarbor Highway — Publicity and Design Services, Premier's Dpt, SA
97 Senator Neville Bonner — N.T. Bonner
101 Sydney Domain — Dpt of Tourism, NSW
107 Crater Lake, Tas. — B.D. Prewer
113 Palm Sunday service of worship and witness, Mt Waverley, Vic., 1973 — B.D. Prewer
123 Brisbane skyline — Dpt of Tourism, Qld

Cover
The Red Cap Gum (Eucalyptus erythrocorys)